The Gardens of Amsterdam Castle Muiderslot

T0306326

Waanders Uitgevers, Zwolle
Rijksmuseum Muiderslot, Muiden

Contents

Four Seasons of Green – Portrait of a Unique Garden

This still life shows a magnificent display of flowers from the castle gardens at Muiderslot. It is full of symbolism and references to the rich history of the castle. Between the flowers in the bouquet we can just see a portrait of writer and poet P.C. Hooft (1581-1647), the castle's most famous resident. Immediately after he moved there, Hooft began planting orchards, gardens and lines of trees around the castle.

The Creation of the Castle Garden

Stronghold

Around 1285 Floris V, Count of Holland and Zeeland, had a stronghold built at a strategic location by the mouth of the river Vecht, close to the Zuyder Zee. In the Middle Ages the site consisted of a small poldered area surrounded by dikes that protected it from water and from enemies. There were two small islands on a sandbank on which the castle – the stronghold – and an outer bailey or outer enclosure stood. Like the castle itself, the outer bailey or outer enclosure, which was surrounded by a wall, also served a defensive purpose. The buildings in the outer bailey were made of wood, reeds and clay so that they could quickly be removed in the event of a siege. The outer bailey had its own drawbridge, a farmhouse and animal stalls, a dairy and a peat store.

A strategic spot

The Vecht was the most important trade route by water to Utrecht. Floris made every ship that passed pay a toll. That earned him a pretty penny, and it also gave him complete control over who entered and left the bishopric of Utrecht. This was a thorn in the side of his greatest enemy, the bishop of Utrecht. He therefore put an end to this after Floris was murdered (in 1296), immediately taking the opportunity to storm and demolish Muiderslot.

Fertile land

Dikes were built along the Vecht and the Zuyder Zee from the early thirteenth century onwards. They protected the hinterland from the water and turned the peat bogs into land suitable for farming or building. The new land, which was constantly drained by windmills to keep it dry, was very fertile.

A new castle on the old foundations

After the murder of Floris V the site where the castle had stood lay abandoned for several decades. In 1363 the bailiff of the Amstel and Gooi region – the count's righthand man – was awarded the lease to the land. Around 1370 Muiderslot was rebuilt on the foundations of Floris's original castle, and a second residential wing was added.

Ramparts and bulwarks

Over the course of the fifteenth century swords and bows and arrows were gradually replaced by guns, against which moats and brick castles offered inadequate protection. In the late sixteenth century earthen ramparts, with bulwarks or bastions projecting outwards, were built to protect Muiden and its castle. The town and castle would be defended from the ramparts. The outer bailey no longer served as a defence. What remained was the farm with its outbuildings, and the gardens.

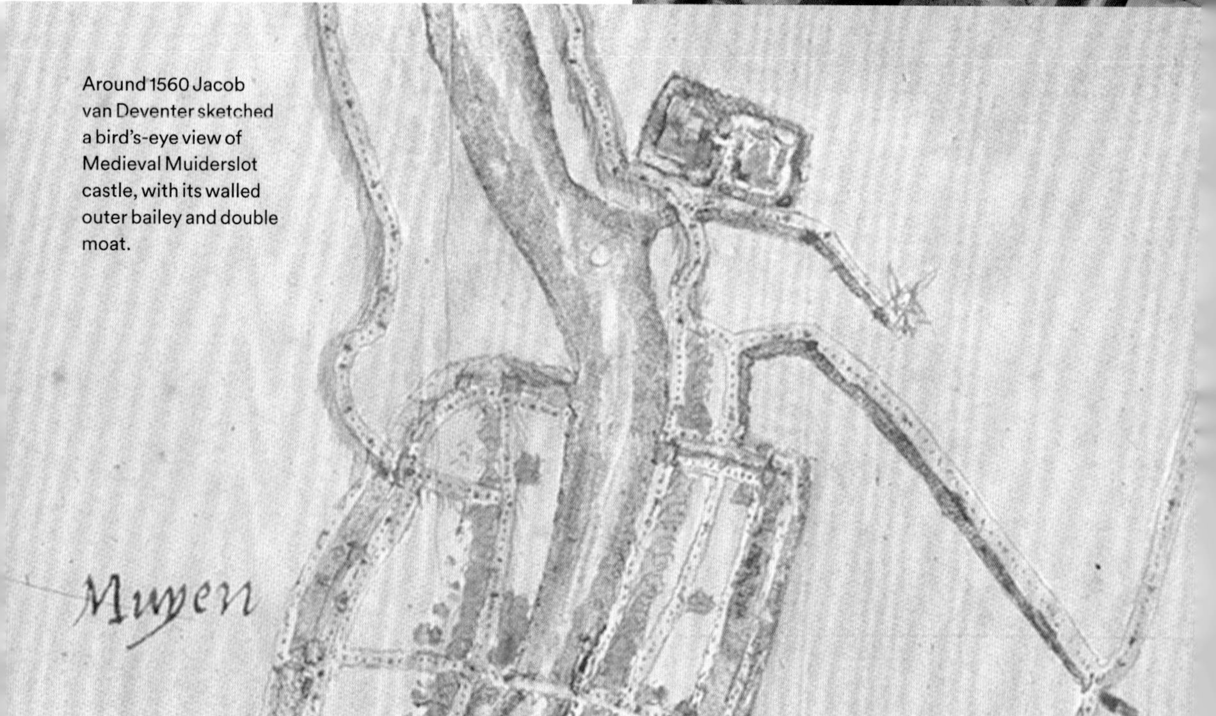

Around 1560 Jacob van Deventer sketched a bird's-eye view of Medieval Muiderslot castle, with its walled outer bailey and double moat.

The Medieval garden

Medieval castles generally had a garden that supplied food for the castle's residents. Besides fruit, vegetables and flowers, castle gardens would also be used to produce medicinal plants, natural dyes and herbs. Flowers with a religious meaning would be used to decorate the altar in the castle's chapel. Food crops like pulses, brassicas and fruit would generally be grown outside the castle walls, on the surrounding land.

Bas Meeuws painted 'Tasteful', a compilation of edible flowers from the castle gardens.

As suggested by the decoration, in the summer the bedpan would be filled with aromatic herbs and scented flowers and placed in the bed to mask any unpleasant odours.

Beautiful and fragrant

From the Middle Ages onwards ladies would carry 'nosegays': small, artistically fashioned wreaths of flowers worn on the body or carried in the hand to keep illness and bad odours at bay. A nosegay would consist of strongly scented flowers and foliage, such as roses and jasmine. The spiral arrangement and binding made them objects of beauty, too.

Medieval statue of Jacoba of Bavaria, Countess of Holland, holding a nosegay (c. 1475).

Castles and estates

Many castles had an estate, which belonged to the castellan. He did not own the land, however. The *heerlijkheid*, or seigneurial estate came with certain seigneurial rights in a certain area. The castellan had the right to the yield from the land, the tolls, the water, the wind and hunting rights. If he leased part of his estate the tenant would have to give him a portion of the yield or pay rent. Seigneurial rights were highly lucrative for the castellan.

Muiderslot from the north-east by Gerrit Berkheyde (ca. 1653-1698).

New seigneurial estates

More and more wealthy townsmen bought estates, and they would often add the name of their new possession to their surname. Estates came with castles, land and status. From the sixteenth century onwards they became pleasant places to relax outside town, with decorative gardens. During the seventeenth century many *regenten* (rulers of the Dutch republic) from Amsterdam bought estates along the Amstel and the Vecht.

A Rural Castle Garden

More luxury at the castle
In 1609 the son of the mayor of Amsterdam, Pieter Corneliszoon Hooft, became the first bailiff who was not from the nobility to move into Muiderslot. A bailiff was an important administrator. Hooft was used to the luxury of his canalside home in Amsterdam, and he expected to have the same comforts at the castle. Embrasures were turned into glazed windows, the walls were whitewashed and new fireplaces were installed. Hooft lived at Muiderslot for almost 40 years.

Portrait of P.C. Hooft (1581-1647) after a 17th-century original by Michiel van Mierevelt.

P.C. Hooft visited his future new workplace and sketched Muiderslot from the north in November 1608.

Gods and mortals enjoying the garden in this painting by Louis de Caullary (c. 1590-1621).

Claes Janszoon Visscher, a friend of P.C. Hooft's, drew Muiderslot Castle in 1617. There are trees around the castle, and the moat and ramparts are covered with undergrowth and reeds.

Country seat by the Vecht

P.C. Hooft was a writer and poet, as were many of his friends. Interest in classical antiquity revived in the seventeenth century. The classic image of the simple country life also took hold in Holland. Gardens became fashionable, the ideal spot to study art and literature, play music, muse on life and discuss classical history, literature and philosophy. Hooft also expected life in the country to be a paradise, as evidenced by the many original and engaging letters he wrote inviting guests to stay at Muiderslot. He often presented his garden and plum orchard as an extra attraction.

Useful trees

There are no known images of Hooft's actual gardens, but his letters give us an impression of his new paradise by the Vecht. Immediately after his appointment he began planting rows of trees on the ramparts. Rows of nut trees, elm and poplars acted as windbreaks, shielding the castle from the strong winds blowing off the Zuyder Zee. Hooft had fruit trees and a plum orchard planted around the castle. Plums were prized for their sweetness. The other decorative fruit trees were cultivated on espaliers that stood against the ramparts.

This painting of a fisherman by Arent Arentszoon (known as Cabel) is the only known image of the plum orchard during the time of P.C. Hooft.

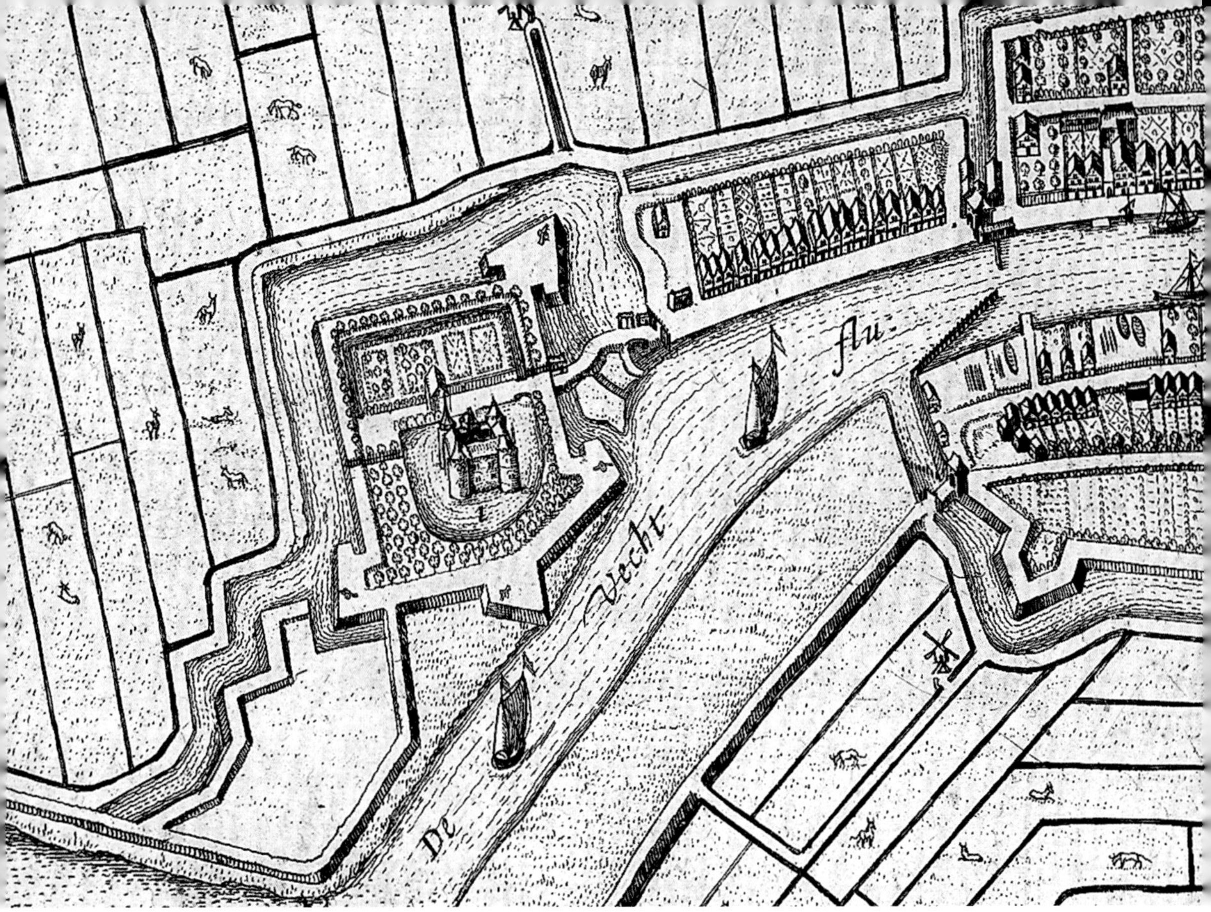

Detail of Muyden, from *Tonneel der steden van Hollandt* by M.Z. Boxhorn, 1632.

Castle gardens

Hooft had neatly arranged gardens and hedges laid out on the site of the former outer bailey, as can be seen in the plan of Muiden in a 1632 atlas of Dutch towns. The gardens are shown schematically, however, so we do not know exactly what they looked like.

Self-sufficient

Muiderslot was both a defensive stronghold and an official residence. Hooft's gardens were therefore both decorative and practical. The castle and its ramparts would provide a military buffer against any attack on Amsterdam. If the castle were besieged the occupants and troops could become entirely self-sufficient, and would at any rate have been able to feed themselves using fruit and vegetables from the garden. Hooft will undoubtedly also have had new and unusual varieties of vegetables in his gardens – artichokes, asparagus, tomatoes and rhubarb – which he could not buy at the local markets.
But the castle also had an official role. Hooft represented the States of Holland, and unexpected or distinguished visitors from the city or the state could always rely on a hospitable welcome at the castle. The neatly arranged garden was also designed to convey a certain impression to important visitors.

Green defences

The trees on the ramparts reinforced the earthen dikes with their roots, acted as windbreaks and supplied wood for a fence to be built in the event of a siege. Alder, ash and willow grew fast and supplied plenty of timber. The dense thorny vegetation on the dikes also held attackers at bay. Leafy trees like elm, oak and nut trees concealed the castle.

Simon de Vlieger painted the ramparts of the castle with their rich vegetation around 1650.

Seventeenth-century flower arranging

Maria Tesselschade Roemersdochter Visscher was a frequent and welcome guest at Muiderslot. During her annual visits to Muiden she and Hooft's daughters would make garlands of flowers to decorate the great hall. Poet Gerbrand Bredero affectionately dubbed her the muse of Hooft's circle of literary friends. The flower arrangers who volunteer to decorate the halls of Muiderslot with seventeenth-century arrangements are her present-day counterparts. They use seasonal materials from the castle gardens.

Flower arrangements Muiderslot

● The new country life

The classics describe Arcadia as a pastoral idyl inhabited by shepherds and nymphs.

Back to the classics

New ideas about the role of nature in the garden and in the home became fashionable in the Low Countries. There was growing interest in the classical ideals of nature, the country life, beauty and harmony as described by Greek and Roman philosophers around the start of the common era. They believed Arcadia was a classical paradise from a lost golden age, a dream of a green land where it is always summer.

A private paradise

After the founding of the United East India Company (VOC) in 1602 new goods began to arrive in Holland. People encountered exotic plants, herbs and spices from overseas for the first time. This changed their outlook on nature, which was much richer and more varied than they had imagined. A new image of the Biblical paradise, the counterpart to the earthly Arcadia of classical antiquity, began to develop. The newly rich would have decorative gardens laid out to create their own earthly paradise.

'Spring', from *Hortus Floridus* by Crispijn de Passe de Jonge (1614).

The garden as a museum

University botanical gardens created for the purposes of study, also known as *horti botanici*, soon began to feature tulip bulbs and other rare plants. Rich people would show them off in their gardens. These gardens, which were often square, would have symmetrical beds with individual topiaried trees, plants and bulbs. Gardens became a kind of outdoor museum, a living art collection. The most beautiful plants and flowers were described and illustrated in *Florilegia* (books of flowers).

Tulipmania

The tulip comes from Asia Minor. In the early to mid-seventeenth century it was the most popular – and the most expensive – flower around. Their love of this exotic species literally went to the heads of the Dutch, and the price of a single tulip bulb eventually rose to the equivalent of an entire canalside house in Amsterdam. Tulips were also popular decorative features in the home, appearing on all kinds of items, including treasure chests and rugs.

Still Life with Vase of Flowers and Pocket Watch by Abraham van Beijeren, early to mid-17th century.

The Gardens of P.C. Hooft

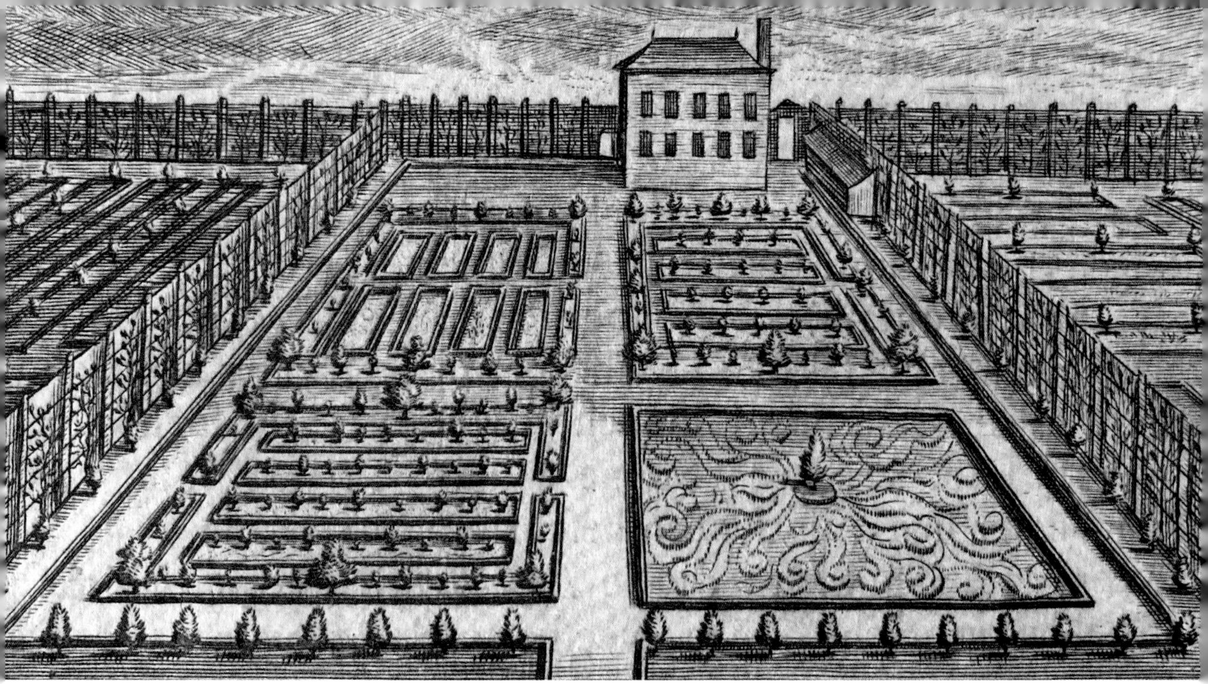

Een Nederlandtse Hof of Tuyn, en bloemperck ('A Dutch Garden, a flower bed')

Arcadia in Holland

Growing trade and prosperity drew many people to the cities in the provinces of Noord- and Zuid-Holland. Urbanisation increased rapidly. Rich citizens, inspired by the classical image of a simple country life, now went in search of peace, relaxation and clean healthy air in the countryside. They bought country estates and country houses outside the city, including along the Amstel and Vecht rivers, and created classical gardens there, just as P.C. Hooft did at Muiderslot.

Hooft on his gardens

Hooft funded his castle gardens himself, and designed them entirely in accordance with his own wishes. He and his family would most often spend time at Muiderslot in the summer. Hooft frequently referred to his gardens in his letters, mentioning the produce his gardener would pick, or inviting his friends to come and pick it themselves. This gives us some idea of the layout and planting of his gardens. There are other sources, such as stories about the gardens in letters from his friends and associates, that tell us more about the classical garden design and about gardening in Hooft's circle.

Title illustration from Jan van der Groen's 1686 book on country life and gardening *Den Nederlandtsen Hovenier, Zijnde het I. Deel van het Vermakelyck Landt-leven.*

The Dutch Garden

Jan van der Groen was gardener to the Prince of Orange. His book *Den Nederlandtsen Hovenier* (1669) describes the art of gardening as practised in Holland in the seventeenth century. The book contains detailed instructions for different types of garden layout, maintenance and a list of popular decorative and useful plants. It also contains an example of a typical Dutch formal garden based on a classical balance of useful plants and decorative plants, emphasising the true essence of a garden, as food and ornament for body and mind.

The Well-provisioned Kitchen after Joachim Beuckelaer (1569) has a hidden message: the depiction of the bible story of Jesus visiting Martha and Mary in the background refers to the importance of feeding the spirit.

Today's gardens

Like the traditional Dutch formal garden, today's reconstruction of Hooft's gardens consists of two more or less square gardens separated by an arbour, or *berceau*. Ladies and gentlemen would be able to admire the gardens through the 'windows' in the hedge, while remaining in the shade themselves. In the seventeenth century, a pale skin untouched by the sun was the ideal of beauty among the elite. To the left of the arbour, just in front of the castle, is the geometrically arranged Herbaceous Garden, and to the right is the reconstruction of the seventeenth-century vegetable garden, the Kitchen Garden.
The gardens of Muiderslot offer today's visitors every opportunity to wander, enjoy, smell and taste everything a garden has to offer, just as they did in Hooft's day.

Section of a map from *Blaeus grooten atlas, oft, Wereltbeschryving* [..] of 1655, with P.C. Hooft's 'grand tour' indicated in red. He travelled from Amsterdam to La Rochelle, Paris, Venice, Rome, Naples and Florence, and returned via Germany.

Grand tour

As a young man, like many other wealthy young men in the seventeenth century, Hooft went on an educational trip, or *grand tour*, to France and Italy. The purpose of the trip was to learn the French and Italian languages and cultures. Hooft also visited gardens during his travels, and was particularly impressed by the Italian garden at Villa Pratolino in Florence. On his return trip through Germany, he might also have been inspired by the famous gardens of merchant and mayor Casper Anckelmann near Hamburg.

Engraving by H.S. Holtzbecker (1610?-1671) in *Hortus Anckelmannius*.

Ideal proportions

The castle gardens were strictly arranged in accordance with the golden ratio. This classical formula encapsulated the ideal proportions in nature, guaranteeing beauty, balance and harmony. Similar systems were also used in architecture in the seventeenth century.

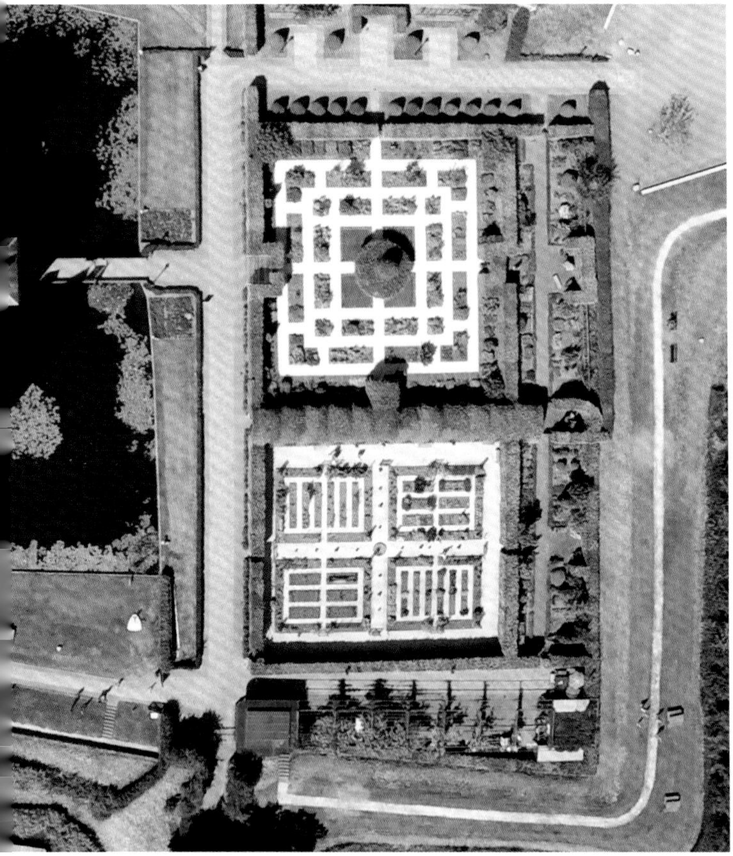

Tulips with special supports in *Hortus Floridus* ('Flower Garden') by Crispijn de Passe de Jonge (1614).

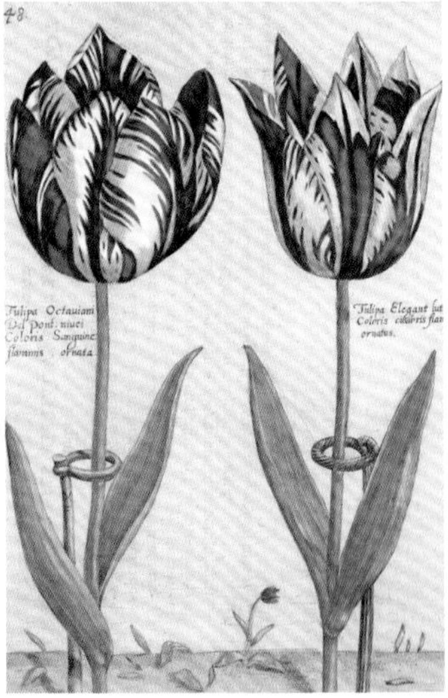

Nature and art

Nature and art met in the Dutch classical garden. The flower garden was a display of the owner's living art collection. Individual trees, flowers and plants were exhibited in decorative flower beds like nature's artworks. Everything was designed to ensure the plants were presented to their best advantage.

Useful and beautiful

The outer beds of the Herbaceous Garden were planted for harvesting, and contained medicinal and edible plants and natural dyes. The inner beds around the lime tree featured decorative plants, with a display of the latest and most expensive flowers in Hooft's day. The beds were raised and the flowers and individual plants were exhibited like garden statues.

Tree of Life

The striking three-tiered lime tree at the centre of the Herbaceous Garden was both a Christian and a secular symbol. It represents the Holy Trinity: Father, Son and Holy Ghost. The tree also symbolised the three layers of society: the clergy, the nobility and the people. The Tree of Life was the heart of the classical garden. Lime blossom has medicinal properties, and can be used to alleviate respiratory problems, as well as providing plenty of nectar and pollen for the bees. It also provided a shady spot, a wonderful place to while away the time.

405
Cc 3

The garden indoors

◀ FLOREAE POMPAE FERCVLVM TVRRITVM: 'portable flower arrangement with tower' in a tinted etching in Giovanni Battista Ferrari's *De Florum cultura* (1633).

▶ IDE VAS ORDINATIS FLORIBVS CONSPICVVM Dd: 'vase with richly perforated lid, to display flowers in an orderly manner' in a tinted etching in Giovanni Battista Ferrari's *De Florum cultura* (1633).

Ingenious vases

The book *De Flora Cultura* was extremely popular in the Low Countries, and it was reprinted a number of times in Amsterdam. Hooft may have seen the book himself. Ferrari describes unique vases with ingenious pipe and drainage systems. These flower holders had several parts, some of them with perforations in an orderly pattern, intended for displaying individual blooms. Ferrari also designed a simpler, more practical version with a removable perforated lid. It could be made in earthenware, silver or porcelain.

Tulip vases

The famous Dutch tulip vases were first made in the mid- to late seventeenth century. The earthenware vases with spouts were made in Delft, and they resemble Chinese porcelain. The earliest spouted vases from Delft are shaped like a tulip, and so they became known as tulip vases. Despite the name, however, they were not only used for tulips, but for all the wonderful blooms that the garden provided.

The Gardens after Hooft

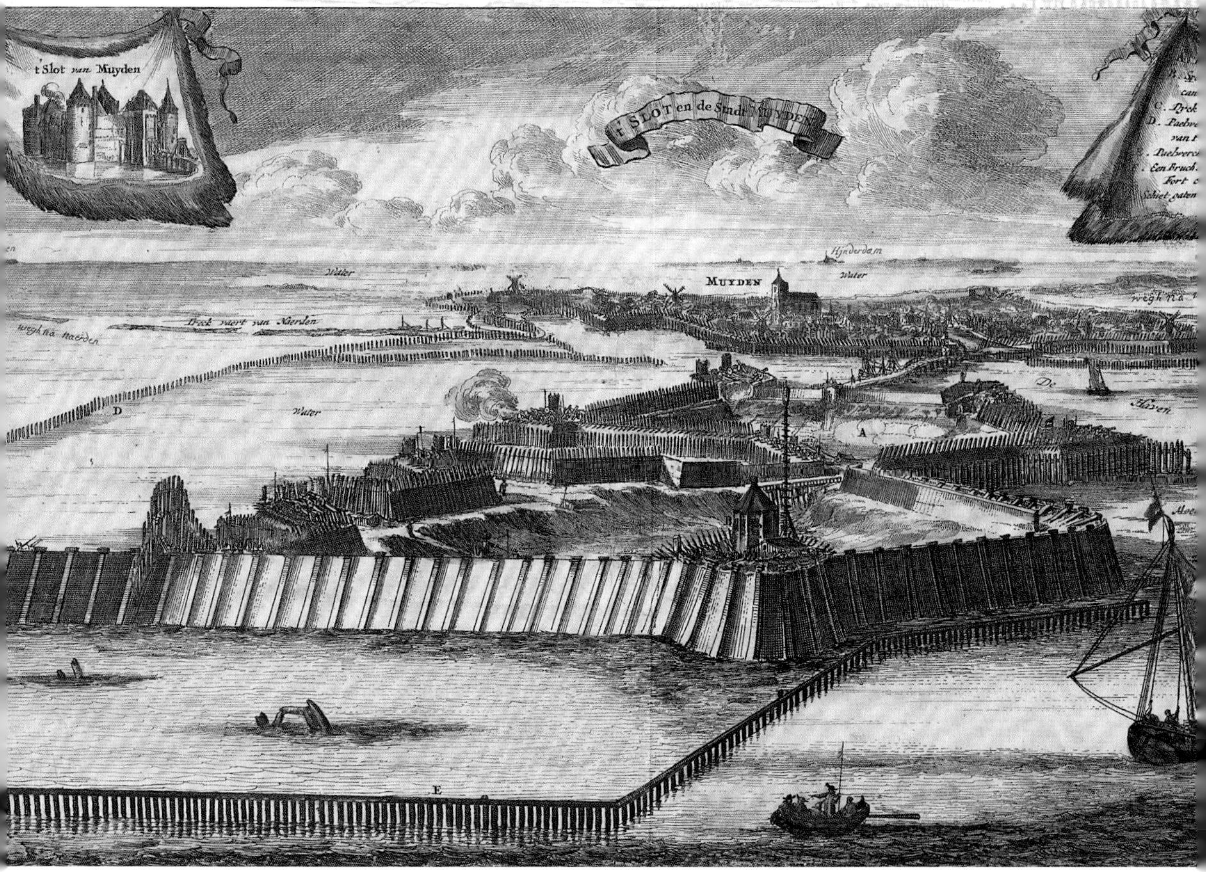

Here, flooding has turned Muiden and the castle into an island. The remains of the garden have been sketched schematically on what remained of the outer bailey.

Hooft's death in 1647 the castle and its gardens remained the property of the States of Holland. Twenty-five years later the French invaded the Low Countries and Muiderslot was converted to a defensive stronghold as a precaution. Over the centuries it was repeatedly adapted to withstand the latest weapons and methods of warfare.

Muiderslot in the early 18th century, with picture windows in the curtain wall, and a revetted island in the moat beneath.

The gardens in the eighteenth century

Later occupants of the castle had gardens too. As far as we can ascertain, the garden always included a combination of useful and decorative plants, depending on the prevailing fashion. Drawings from the eighteenth century show that the gardens were used predominantly for pleasure, with decoratively cut hedges around the outer bailey and the moat, landscaped paths and decorative gardens behind the castle. The embrasures in the southern defensive wall had been expanded into large windows that afforded a fine view of the garden.

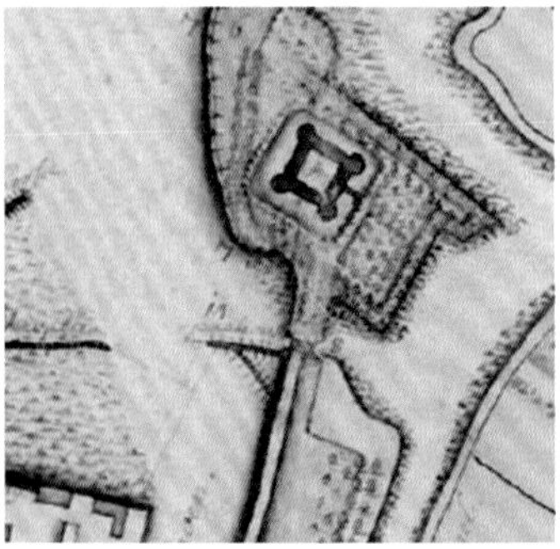

On Prévost's map (1726) the ramparts have been planted and there are clear avenue structures and gardens in front of the castle.

Silent witnesses

The amount of time, money and energy the castellan invested in the gardens will have varied. We know for sure, however, that Hooft took a personal interest in the garden. A few drawings of the castle and its surroundings have survived from other periods, and bills for maintenance work refer to repairs to fences and outhouses, among other things.

This painting from the early to mid-18th century shows the ramparts planted with elm, which could withstand the salty sea air.

Muiderslot without a castellan

In 1787 marauding patriots (who rebelled against the ruling powers) vandalised both the castle and its grounds. All public officials lost their post when the Dutch Republic fell. The bailiff of the Gooi region, who lived at Muiderslot Castle, was no exception. In 1795 the last castellan left Muiderslot and the grounds and gardens were abandoned. From then on the castle was used only for military purposes. A caretaker and his family lived there. They had a small vegetable garden in the outer enclosure.

Muiderslot viewed from the south in 1863. The South Tower no longer has a pointed roof, though it does still have the unique slate sundial, which adorns the tower to this day.

Outer bailey of Muiderslot around 1820.

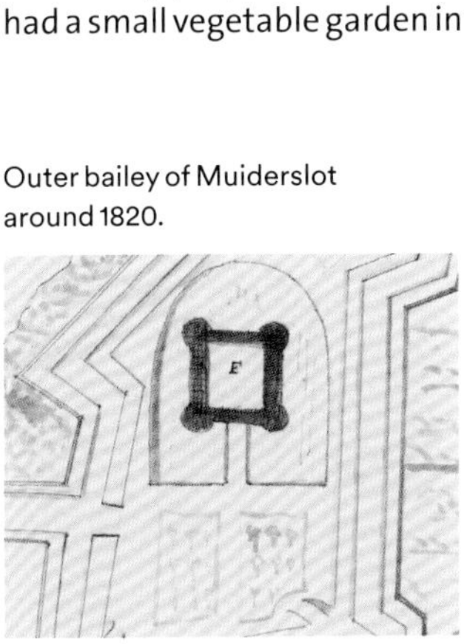

Outer bailey of Muiderslot around 1858.

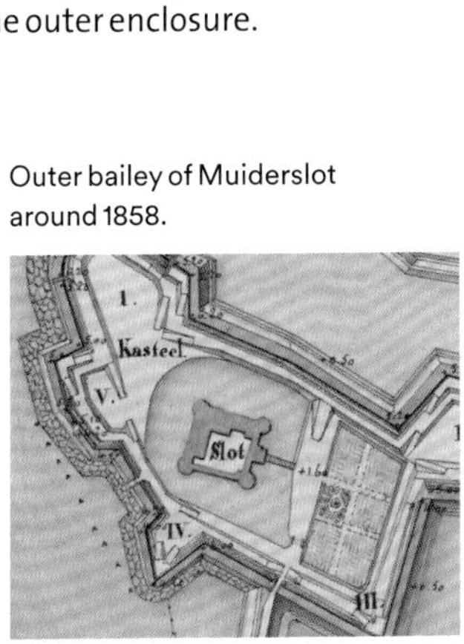

Castle delicacies

De verstandige kock of sorghvuldige huyshoudster was the leading cookery book in the Netherlands in the seventeenth century. It gives a good impression of what was roasted, braised, boiled and baked in the kitchens of the wealthy at that time. The book has a lot of recipes involving produce grown in one's own vegetable garden.

Raw artichoke salad

Take young artichokes, remove all the leaves and scoop out the choke (or 'beard') with a pointed spoon. Ensure that the artichoke heart is clean. Slice thinly and eat with pepper, salt, sugar, oil and vinegar.

Plum jelly

2 kg blue-black plums
750 ml apple juice
30 g ground cinnamon
30 g ground ginger
15 g ground cloves
15 g ground laos root (galangal)
15 g ground nutmeg
juice of 1 lemon
approx. 750 g sugar for 1 litre of jelly
To make plum jelly with less sugar, use preserving sugar and follow the instructions on the pack.

Stone the plums and place them in a stainless steel pan with the apple juice. Bring to the boil and simmer gently. Press the boiled plums through a sieve and add the lemon juice. To each pound of sieved plum mixture add 30 g cinnamon, 30 g ginger, 15 g cloves, laos root and and nutmeg, and stir well. Then add approx. 750 g sugar to every litre of jelly. Boil vigorously and pour a spoonful of hot compote onto a plate. Tilt the plate to check the thickness. If it remains in place the jelly is thick enough. If it does not, return it to the pan and boil for a little longer. Pour the plum jelly into clean jars.

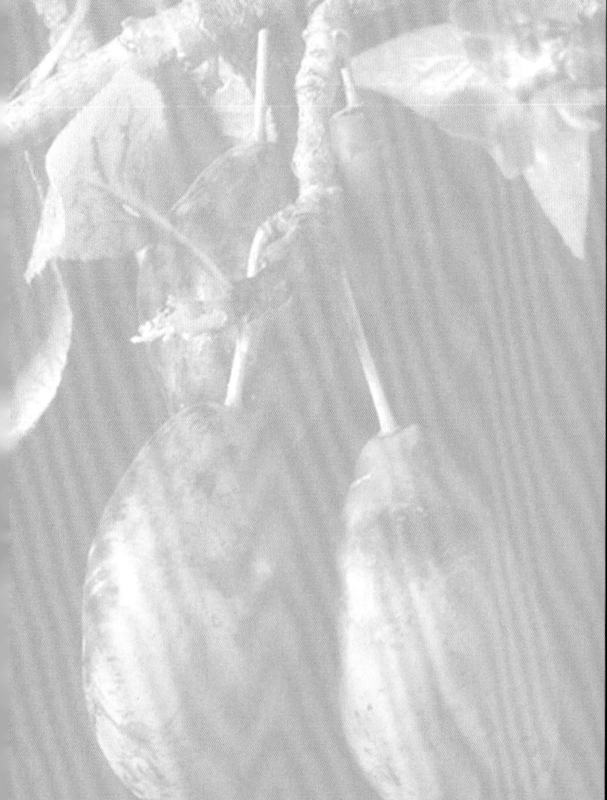

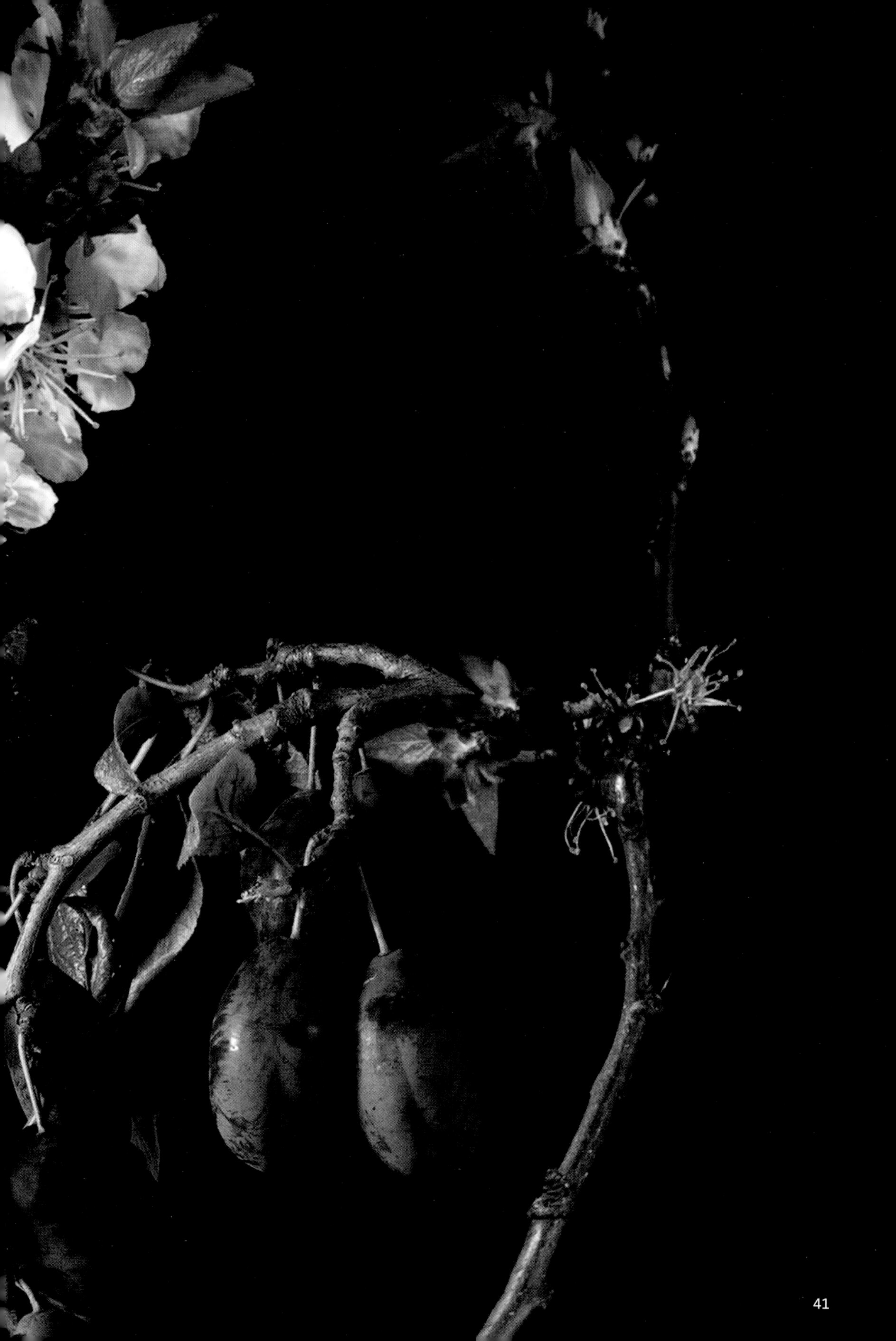

The garden on the table

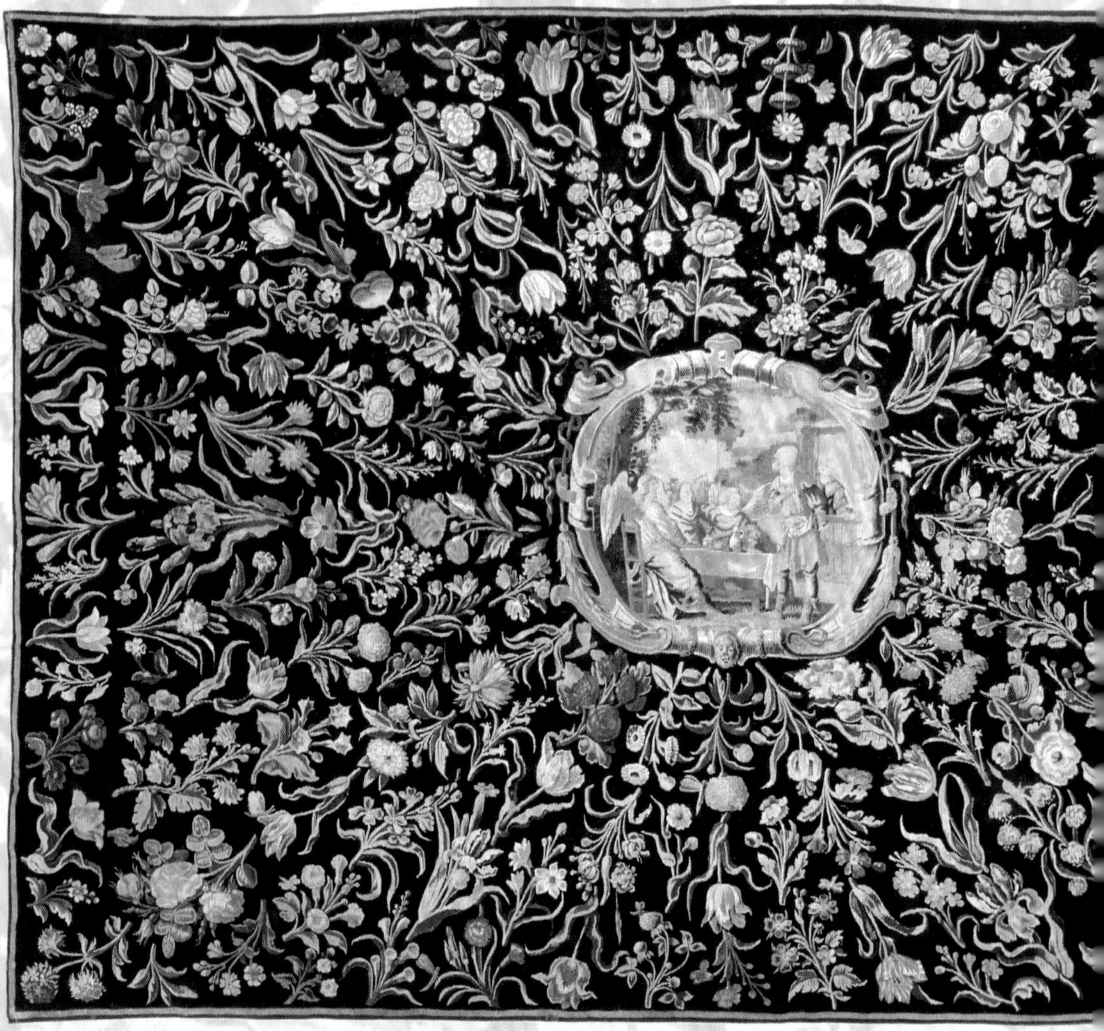

Tulip tablecloth, mid-17th century.

In this early 17th-century painting by Frans Francken de Jonge (et al.) even the picnic rug used by the shepherds in Arcadia is strewn with roses, pansies, periwinkles and fragrant rosemary.

Table decorations

Like the rooms of the castle, the table would also be decorated using real flowers, or a tablecloth with a floral motif. Tablecloths from the time provide a lot of information about how tables were set for dinner in the seventeenth century. Muiderslot has a unique tulip tablecloth featuring flowers scattered around a central medallion, showing how the table would be scattered with flowers and greenery for their scent, their cooling effect and to keep insects away.

Flowers with taste

Flowers were used for decoration and for flavour. Salads would be made using dandelion, sorrel and radish leaves, and flavoured with bugloss, rose, marigold and borage flowers The Second Book of Cookery, an English cookery book published in 1641, contains a recipe for a 'grand' salad with a floral garnish: little trees made of rosemary hung with morello cherries.

Pyramids of fruit

A dish itself could also be a decorative feature. Pies were made in the form of peacocks, swans and turkeys. Candied fruit and sugared flowers and almonds would be presented in pyramids featuring several layers of fruit with flowers and foliage between.

Sugary sweet

The garden would provide most of the ingredients of the meal. Nuts and fruit would be candied immediately after harvesting, or made into jam. Hooft wisely chose to plant a plum orchard, as the high sugar content of the preserved fruit made them a popular alternative to honey, or to expensive sugar loaves imported from Brazil.

A 'Grand Sallet' from *The Second Book of Cookery* (1641): The salad consists of sorrel, mustard, watercress, dandelions, spinach and radish, mixed with large capers, dates, currant, figs and blanched almonds. The half lemons, supporting little rosemary trees full of cherries, provide the finishing touch.

Garden centrepieces

On special occasions the dishes on the table would be laid out like a garden. During large receptions the dessert would be served in the form of an exquisite garden, with impressive sugarwork arbours, piles of fruit, sugared edible flowers, herbs and foliage. The garden dessert would be the absolute highlight of the festivities. Such grand banquets would often be served at a wedding, for example.

Sweet paradise

The 'sugar garden' remained a favourite in the eighteenth century, as can clearly be seen in a painting of the table decorations for the golden wedding anniversary of Gerrit Hooft and Hester Hinlopen (1757). The centrepiece was an illuminated temple made of sugar. An olive wreath hung inside the temple, above a miniature bridal couple made of sugar. The temple was scattered with fresh flowers and aromatic herbs.

From Military Site to Museum

New gardens for the museum
Muiderslot became a museum in 1878. The fortifications around the castle served a military purpose until after the Second World War. A map from 1950 shows how the property was divided between the Ministry of War and the Ministry of Education, Arts and Sciences. The Ministry of War did not in fact transfer the fortifications and outer bailey to the museum until 1954. The military buildings were demolished and the ramparts were planted with elm. The museum made plans for the reconstruction of P.C. Hooft's gardens and plum orchard.

Hedges and topiary gardens were laid out around the site of bunker B after it had been demolished. From 1956 onwards the Herb Garden was created in the area in front of former bunker B.

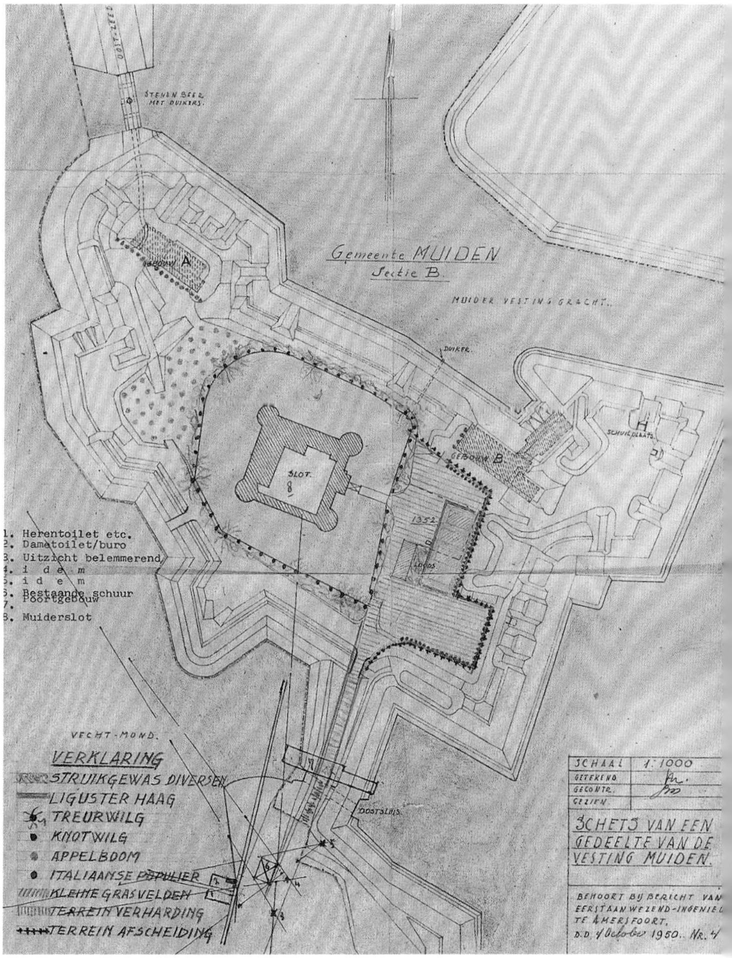

The dotted line on this 1950 map shows the boundary between the military and museum site. The north and east bastions now have bunkers (A and B).

The Herbaceous Garden

The Herbaceous Garden was laid out where the military buildings had once stood. It was surrounded by a hedge and a topiary garden. It includes elements of different styles of garden: Medieval turf seats, Baroque parterre planting and modern gravel paths (made of a mix of ground rubble, incl. bricks and roof tiles). In the early 1980s the Herbaceous Garden was restored in accordance with the ideas of the time, and transformed into a Dutch Garden. The lawns were reduced in size, the turf seats were removed and the dimensions of the beds were converted from metres to Amsterdam feet (=28.3 cm). Yew was planted around the beds, which were planted in a largely early-seventeenth-century style. The plants were now divided into useful and decorative, as in Hooft's day. Soft fruits – mulberries, medlars, hazel and quince – were planted in the corners.

In 2015 the yew hedges were removed because of a fungal infection, and replaced by toe boards.

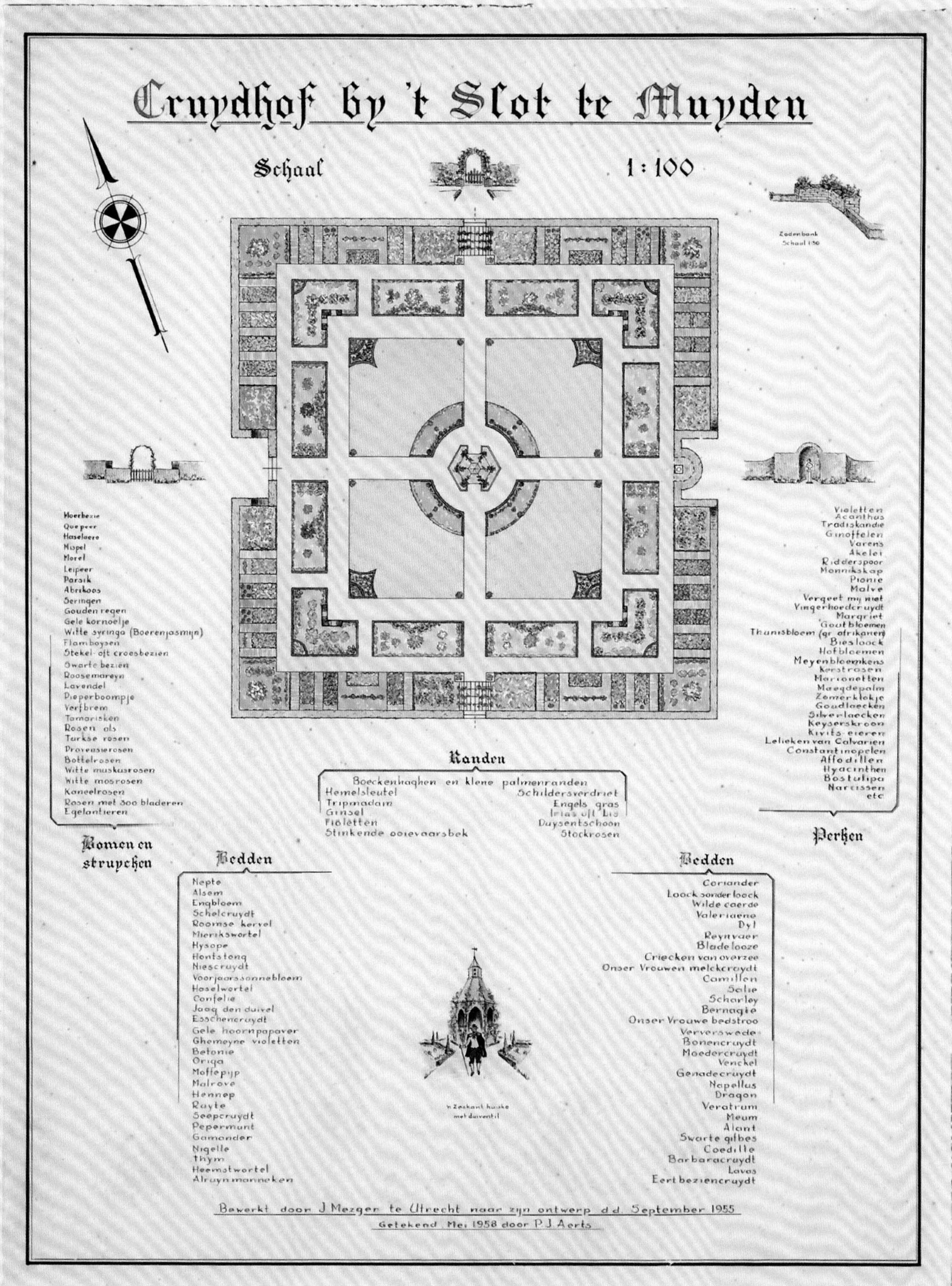

Design for the 'Cruydhof' (Herb Garden) by J. Mezger and A. Kipp, 1956.

A Dutch vegetable garden

In 2000 the restoration of Hooft's gardens was finally completed with the reconstruction of the Kitchen Garden. This was the first reconstruction in the Netherlands of a formal vegetable garden typical of Noord- and Zuid-Holland provinces. Like the Herbaceous Garden, this garden is small, with a symmetrical design, a classical aspect ratio and it is divided into areas for different varieties of vegetables, some of them largely forgotten.

The vegetable garden is divided into four segments, for brassicas, root vegetables, mixed vegetables and leafy vegetables. To keep the soil fertile, the crops are rotated clockwise through the four quarters of the garden each year, as recommended in Jan van der Groen's seventeenth-century gardener's manual.

Forgotten vegetables

Old varieties of vegetables are less cultivated than more recent vegetables, and are closer to their wild ancestors. As a result, they are often more bitter and strongly flavoured. The flavour of the white icicle radish is similar to that of wasabi, for instance, and it can really make your ears pop! The forgotten vegetables have a firmer texture and therefore take longer to cook. Some vegetables, like asparagus, purslane and rhubarb, are bleached under clay and glass cloches to make them less bitter and easier to prepare.

The Giant Radish, painting by an anonymous early 17th-century artist.

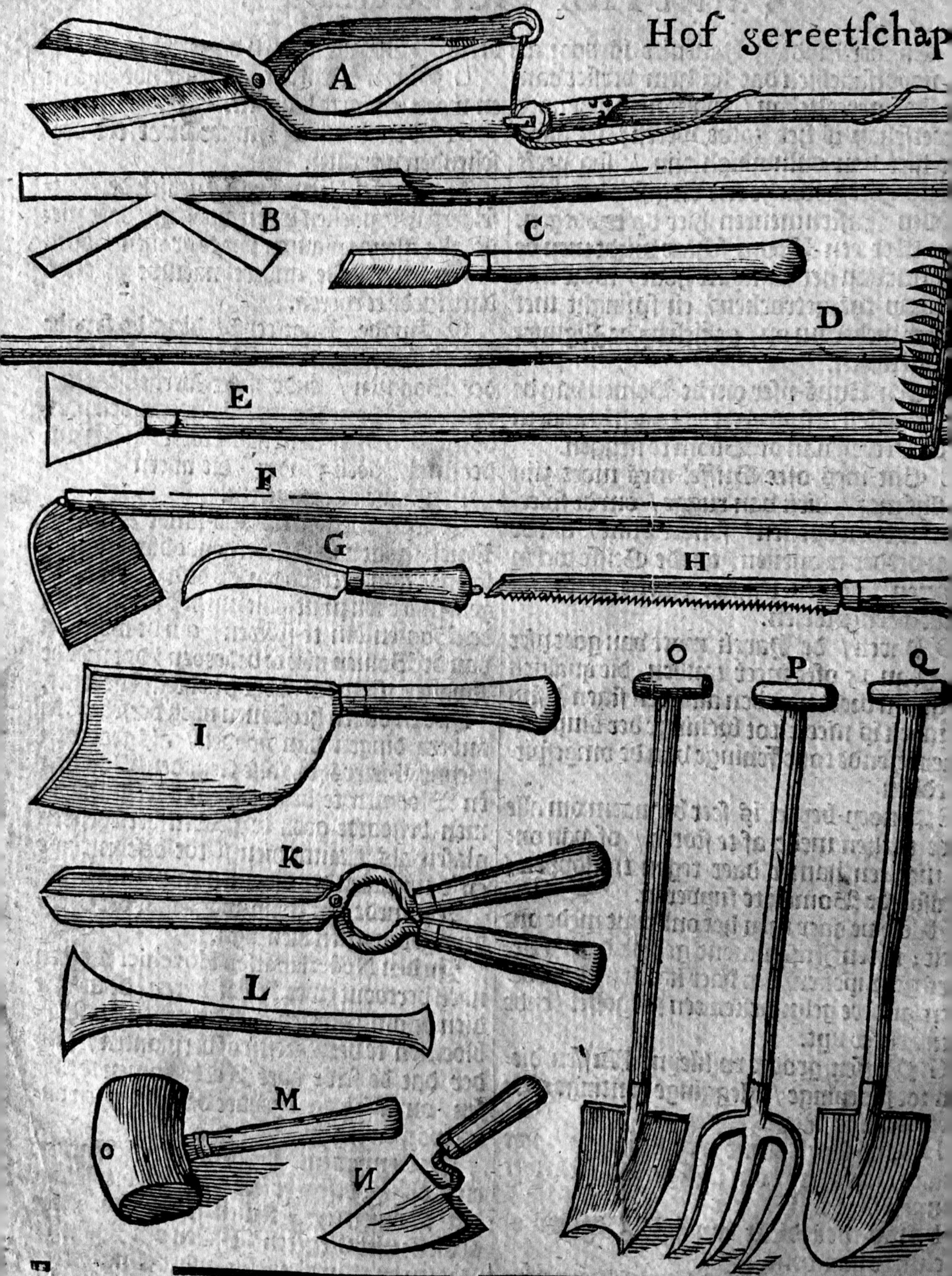
Hof gereetschap
A
B
C
D
E
F
G
H
I
K
L
M
N
O
P
Q

Gardening seventeenth-century style

The gardens are looked after by volunteers, known as *warmoezeniers*. They plant and tend the gardens, just as the castle gardeners did in the seventeenth century. And like then, they took work according to the lunar cycle. Each of the vegetables can best be sown, planted or harvested when the moon is new, full or waxing. The garden calendar at the back of the book reveals some of the castle garden's secrets.

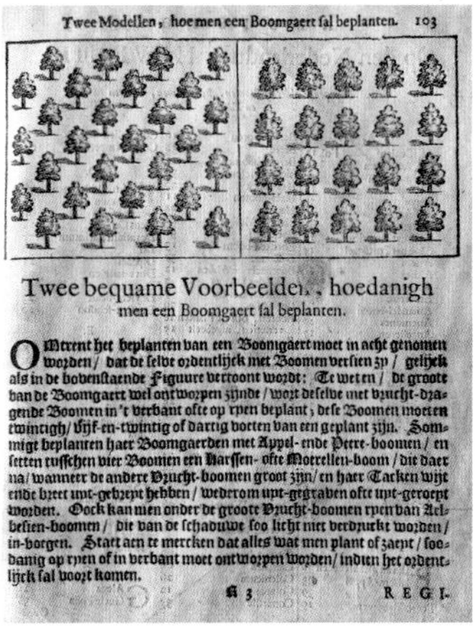

Twee Modellen, hoe men een Boomgaert sal beplanten. 103

Twee bequame Voorbeelden, hoedanigh men een Boomgaert sal beplanten.

OMtrent het beplanten van een Boomgaert moet in acht genomen worden / dat de selve ordentlijck met Boomen versien zy / gelijck als in de bovenstaende Figuure vertoont wordt: Te weten / de groote van de Boomgaert wel ontworpen zijnde / wort deselve met vrucht-dragende Boomen in 't verbant ofte op ryen beplant; dese Boomen moeten twintigh / vijf-en-twintig of dartig voeten van een geplant zijn. Sommige beplanten haer Boomgaerden met Appel- ende Peere-boomen / en setten tusschen vier Boomen een Karssen- ofte Morellen-boom / die daer na / wanneer de andere Vrucht-boomen groot zijn / en haer Tacken wijt ende breet uyt-gebreyt hebben / wederom uyt-gegraven ofte uyt-geroeyt worden. Oock kan men onder de groote Vrucht-boomen ryen van Aelbesien-boomen / die van de schaduwe soo licht niet verdruckt worden / in-borgen. Staet aen te mercken dat alles wat men plant of zaeyt / soodanig op ryen of in verbant moet ontworpen worden / indien het ordentlijck sal voort komen.

K 3 REGI-

Living heritage

The restoration of the orchard was completed in 2006. Hooft's famous plum orchard had many historical varieties of plum, from the Mirabelle de Nancy to the Betuwe zwetschge. The trees are half-standard, making pruning and picking easier. All very convenient for Hooft's guests and today's visitors! The more functional farmer's orchards had only standard trees, as young cattle would be allowed to graze under them.

The gardens and plum orchard at Muiderslot are the museum's living heritage. They give visitors an impression of the seventeenth-century botanical heritage, with its great wealth of species and varieties. Each year, in the first weekend of September, visitors to Muiderslot can taste the plums and other delicious produce from the castle gardens.

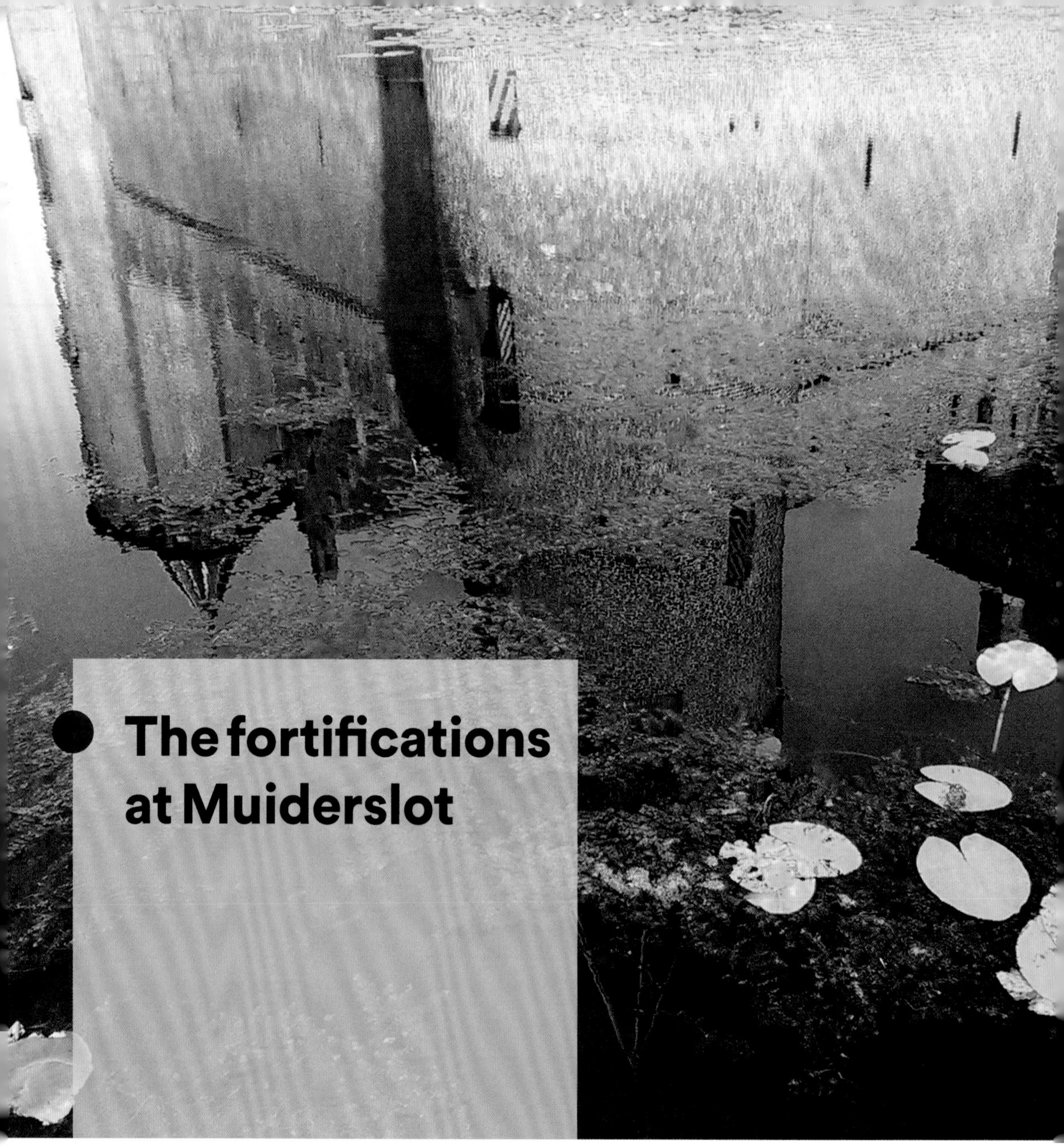

The fortifications at Muiderslot

Castle in the water

Muiderslot is surrounded by water. For centuries, water played a crucial role in the defence of the castle, and later also of Amsterdam. After gunpowder and cannons were invented, the castle moat no longer provided enough protection. From around 1570 the line of defence around the castle was moved and expanded with earthen ramparts, and later with protruding bastions. The fortifications were adapted repeatedly in response to developments in weaponry and warfare.

View of the plum orchard and Water Shield from the West Tower.

Water as a weapon

From the seventeenth century onwards the Dutch developed a unique system of defences employing water as a weapon. When there was a threat of attack, certain areas were inundated with water that was too deep to walk or ride through, but not deep enough for a boat. From 1629 to 1952 the stronghold of Muiderslot was part of several of these water-based defence systems, including *Vesting Holland and the Stelling van Amsterdam* – a line of defences that is currently a UNESCO World Heritage Site.

Muiderslot around 1930.

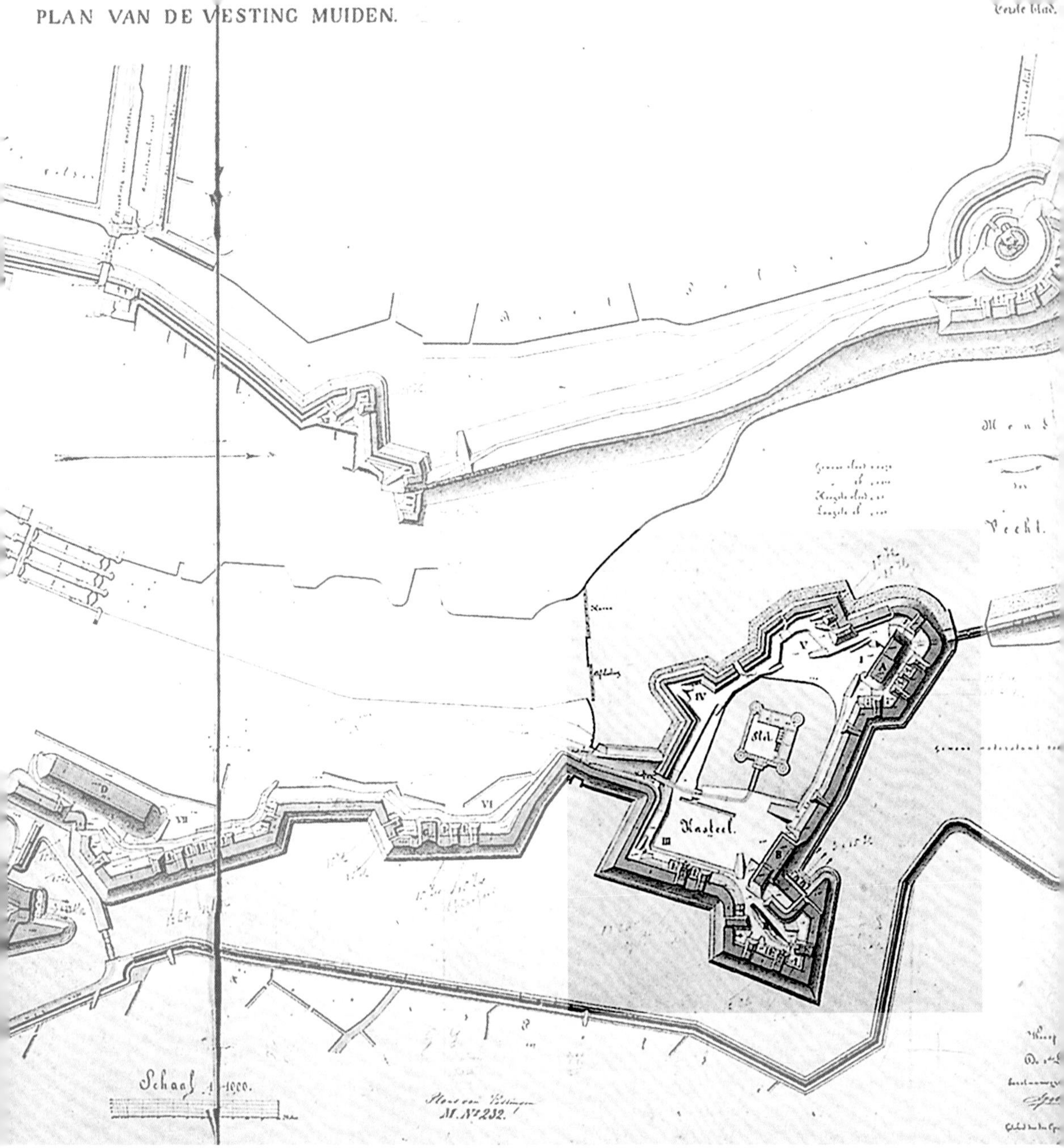

Green housing

The ramparts and bastions were upgraded over the centuries. The defences would be manned at times of war. When the fortress was last modernised in 1877 two bombproof brick bunkers or casemates were built as barracks for the troops: bunker A in the east rampart of the plum orchard behind the castle and bunker B in the east rampart in front of the castle. The old moat around the outer bailey was almost completely filled in.

The completely modernised fortifications of Muiden and the 'Castle', here referring to Muiderslot and bunkers A and B, with a small piece of moat along the outer bailey, in 1877. Some of bunker B has been preserved and thoroughly restored (now the casemate).

Museum ramparts

The nineteenth-century fortifications and casemates were demolished in 1955 to create space for the reconstruction of P.C. Hooft's gardens and orchard. This removed the start of the *Nieuwe Hollandse Waterlinie* and *Stelling van Amsterdam* defences. The fortifications around Muiderslot were also restored to their seventeenth-century state.

Aerial photograph from 1957.

Say it with flowers!

In the seventeenth century bouquets of flowers reflected the status of one's garden. Skilfully arranged bouquets were made in accordance with strict rules. The less striking, more common flowers formed the basis, while the most attractive blooms were artfully positioned amongst and around them in predetermined ratios, with their heads facing outwards. The stalks were concealed with leaves, and bound together so the bouquet could easily be carried.

FASCICVLVS FLORVM ARTIFICIOSVS: 'artistic bouquet of flowers' in a tinted engraving in Giovanni Battista Ferrari, *De Florum cultura* (1633).

dhof
SIERPLANTEN

Four seasons gardening 17th-century style

The seasons had a great impact on life and gardening in the seventeenth century. The jobs that needed to be done each month were determined by the movements of the moon and stars and the positions of the planets.

Winter

January

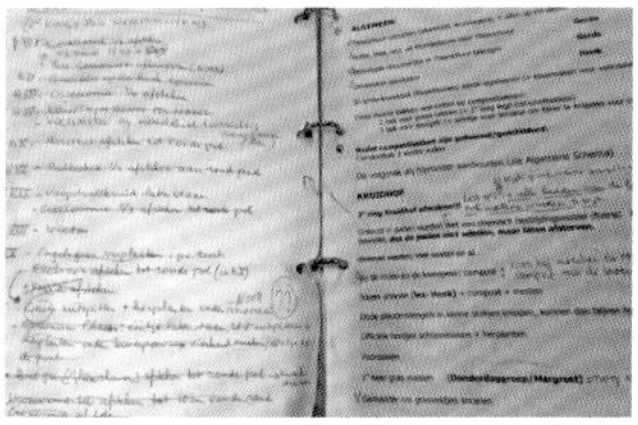

- Compile lists of plants and seeds to order
- Check viability of last year's seeds

- Clean and repair tools ready for use

February

- Add gravel etc. to paths and earth to beds
- Remove seeding weeds such as draba and chickweed
- Do not dig: tidy beds just before sowing/planting

[Late February]
- Sow/ plant broad beans
- With luck, the first crocuses will be in bloom

March

Draw up growing plan for Kitchen Garden, with sowing and planting dates as given in gardening book Den Nederlandtsen Hovenier (1669):
- Sow at new moon
- Germinate seeds and plant out in gardens
- Plant root crops when moon waning

NB: guidelines subject to weather.

- Tidy asparagus and rhubarb beds, turn over, add compost and place bleaching pots over plants
- Place wild potatoes in a cool place to sprout

NB: in Hooft's day the wild potato was grown merely for decoration.

Harvest any leeks, parsnips, root parsley and brassicas that are still edible

- Sow peas and field peas
- Plant out onions and shallots
- Peg out gauze over beds to keep birds off

NB: only if there is no frost!

- Sow lettuce, parsley, beets, chervil, brassicas and endives in cold frames

NB: keep windows closed, mark with name tags

- Set out willow climbing frames for runner beans and tomatoes
- Work compost into beds
- Prune and fertilise roses

- Allow foliage on flowering bulbs and tubers to die back: do not cut back!

- Divide and replant perennials like acanthus and dragon arum in Herbaceous Garden

April

- Blossom on fruit trees and in plum orchard

[From early April:]
- Plant out new cuttings of acephala group brassicas
- Tie plants up if any wind damage is sustained

NB: do not put the roots of old brassicas on the compost heap!

- Check weather forecasts and farmers' sayings in the *Enkhuizer Almanak* (published since the late 16th century). This almanac contains information on the coming year, including a detailed schedule of holidays and markets, astronomical information and weather predictions. [www.enkhuizeralmanak.nl]

- Check phases of moon and suitable sowing and planting days in the Maria Thun Biodynamic Calendar [www.christofoor.nl or in the App Store: *Maria Thun Biodynamic Calendar*]

- Sow summer flowers
- Sow lettuce, parsley, beets, chervil and maize in cold frames (windows closed)
- Sow carrots, root parsley and parsnip in open ground
- Sow basil and tagetes under cloches
- Sow and germinate tomatoes, cucumbers, courgettes, pumpkins and chilli peppers in a light, heated room/greenhouse and harden in a cold frame.

[From late April:]
- Take dahlias, marvel of Peru, canna and crinum out of winter storage and plant
- Take potted plants such as agapanthus out of winter storage and pot on, fertilise and remove foliage

NB: pot plants on into a pot one size bigger!

- Sow annuals, including marigolds and California poppy

- Plant out and water seedlings of dill, hollyhocks, feverfew etc.

- Sow rapa varieties of brassica

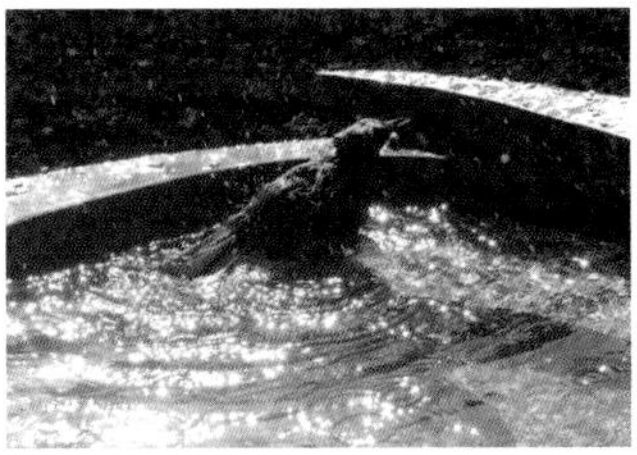

- Prepare castle's facilities for flower arranging volunteers

- Water regularly (including water feature, for birds!)

NB: Keep watering cans full so the water can warm up in the sun.

May

- Plant annuals in open ground

May

- Lighten lettuce under special low bleaching pots
- Harvest last brassicas and bleached rhubarb

NB: Bleached rhubarb is less bitter!

After Ice Saints' Days (11-14/15 May) and if warm enough:

- Sow runner beans along willow supports
- Sow French beans
- Plant out cucumber, courgettes, summer squash, pumpkins, tomatoes, maize and chilli peppers

June

- Train field peas
- Tie up broad beans and check for blackfly
- Pick chard, weed, turn over soil and add compost and bentonite (clay mineral)

- Plant out seedlings like tagetes in all sections of garden
- Lightly rake compost into all sections

- Harvest asparagus until Saint John's Day – the longest day (24 June)
- Regularly pick broad beans, field peas and rhubarb

NB: In the Middle Ages midsummer was celebrated on 24 June, Saint John's Day. Since the introduction of the Gregorian calendar around 1700, 21 June has been regarded as the longest day, but midsummer celebrations continue to be associated with Saint John.

- Sow late brassicas in beds at end of month
- Sow rapa varieties of brassica, sugarloaf chicory and fennel
- Sow autumn endives after Saint John's Day

- Allow sweet briar flowers to die off in order to produce rosehips

July

- Deadhead flowering plants and cut away dead stalks

- Tie up tomatoes, cucumbers and courgettes, top the plants at the desired height and thin out

- Pick artichokes before they flower

August

- Keep picking cucumbers, courgettes and summer squash so the plants continue producing

- Plant out leafy vegetable seedlings when they are big enough

- Cut back perennial herbs like sage, rosemary and lavender after they flower (spring 2/3; summer 1/3)

- Prune beech hedges, arbour and three-tiered lime

September

- Cut back comfrey
- Pick some of the peas, French beans, field peas and broad beans and dry for seeds

- Plant out leeks
- Thin out turnips to 10-20 cm apart
- After onion and shallot leaves have died back, pull up onions and leave to dry on bed

NB: Onion and shallot leaves are not suitable for the compost heap, and should be disposed of by other means!

- First plums harvested for plum liqueur and other specialities.

- First weekend of September: plum time at Muiderslot

- Prune plum trees after harvesting

October

- Leave as much vegetation as possible in beds to protect the soil

- Spring seems to return briefly when the autumn crocus flowers

NB: Highly toxic!

- At the end of the season put dahlias, lily of the Nile and cannas into winter storage, ensuring they are protected from mice and frost

NB: Dry dahlia tubers first!

- Leave dead cardoon flower heads and rosehips as food for the birds

- Harvest the seeds of the castor oil plant to make a laxative

NB: Toxic if used to excess!

November

- Empty and clean watering cans and hang in shed

Apply fertiliser/compost and lime to cyclamens and beech arbour

December

- Winter is coming

- The garden is dormant

- Prune grapevines during dormancy

Winter

Colofon

Published by
Waanders Uitgevers, Zwolle
Rijksmuseum Muiderslot, Muiden

Authors
Henk Boers & Yvonne Molenaar
with the assistance of
Majie Goedhart
Noor Westrik
Gerda van de Hoef
Nannette de Freese
Anneke Lutgendorff
Hans Barendse

Editors
Ben Reef, Cécile Brvar

Copy editor
Loes Visch

Translation
Sue McDonnell

Design
Harald Slaterus

Printing and lithography
Wilco Art Books, Amersfoort

ISBN 978 94 6262 289 0
NUR 425

A Dutch edition is also available
ISBN 978 94 6262 288 3

www.waandersdekunst.nl
www.muiderslot.nl

Photo credits
All images and rights belong to Rijksmuseum Muiderslot, except for:

Collection Algemeen Rijks Archief 56(b)
Collection Amsterdam Museum 10(o)
© Annemarie den Dekker 69(b)(ro)
© Bas Meeuws 4-5, 9, 11, 19, 30-31, 38-39, 41, 50(b), cover
© Beemflights 28
Collection FAI - Castello di Masino, Caravino 32, 33, 59
© Flying Focus 6
Galerie Sanct Lucas, Wenen (2018) 43
© Henk Boers 48(o), 66(o)
© IJsfontein 8(b)
© Kupferstichkabinett der Staatliche Museen zu Berlin - Preußischer Kulturbesitz 27
© Manon Schreuder 60, various photos 62-71
© Mike Bink Fotografie 61(b)
© Monique Hellemons 29(b), 62(b), cover
Collection Nationaal Archief 37(o)
Noord-Hollands Archief, Collectie Provinciale Atlas 37(o)
Rijksmuseum Amsterdam 20, 21(o), 24, 51(o)
© Robert Mulder 44(b), 58, 65(o)
© Sandra Buijs 51(ro), 64(l), 68(o)
Collection Stapleton, © Bridgeman Images 21(b), 29(o)
Stockholm University Art Collections 17
Collection Universiteitsbibliotheek Amsterdam 8(o), 13
Collection Universiteitsbibliotheek Utrecht 26
© Yvonne Molenaar 22, 33(o), 34, 44(o), 48(b), 51(b), 63(o), 65(b), 66(b), 67(o), 69(b)